3.-

This *Wealth Transformation Journal*
belongs to

_____

Wealth Success Series

Wealth
Transformation
Journal

How One Word Can Change
Your Future, One Day At a Time

Kamin Samuel, MS, MA

WORDS HAVE LIFE
P R E S S
Los Angeles, CA

Words Have Life Press
7785 Sunset Blvd
Los Angeles, CA, 90046, USA

Contact the author:
www.KaminSamuel.com

ISBN: 978-0-9800223-8-4

First Edition, First Printing

Dedication

To all of my amazing clients who share their lives with me and are willing to let go of the past and choose wealth...and to all of you.

Table of Contents

Part I - About *Wealth* 9

The *Wealth* Exercise 11

Why *Wealth* 13

Summary *Wealth* Checklist.......................... 23

Part 2 - The Journal 25

My *Wealth* Intentions.................................. 27

Wealth Qualities... 35

Week 1 Wealth Intention 37

Week 2 Wealth Intention 53

Week 3 Wealth Intention 69

Week 4 Wealth Intention 85

Week 5 Wealth Intention 101

Week 6 Wealth Intention 117

Week 7 Wealth Intention 133

Week 8 Wealth Intention 149

Notes.. 167

About the Author.. 173

Part I - About *Wealth*

What I needed to learn was the proactive use of my imagination. And once I'd learned that skill, the first task was to begin imagining the vision of who I wanted to be.

Steve Chandler

The *Wealth* Exercise

The Ideal Method for Building a Wealth Consciousness

Perhaps you are saying as you read this chapter, 'I need wealth and success.' This is what you do: Repeat for about five minutes to yourself three or four times a day, "Wealth. Success." These words have tremendous power. They represent the inner power of the subconscious mind. Anchor your mind on this substantial power within you; then condition and circumstances corresponding to their nature and quality will be manifested in your life. You are not saying, 'I am wealthy,' you are dwelling on real powers within you. There is no conflict in the mind when you say, 'Wealth.' Furthermore, the feeling of wealth will well up within you as you dwell on the idea of wealth.

The feeling of wealth produces wealth; keep this in mind at all times. Your subconscious mind is like a bank, a sort of universal financial institution. It magnifies whatever you deposit or impress upon it whether it is the idea of wealth or of poverty. Choose wealth."

From *The Power of Your Subconscious Mind* (Bantam, 2000, page 114)

Why *Wealth*

I first discovered "The Wealth Exercise" around 1997. I was just starting a long journey of recovery back from bankruptcy and foreclosure. I knew that my financial demise had started in my mind with my thoughts and beliefs so I began a quest to discover how to change both. You can read all the gory details in my book *Increase Your Abundance Starting Today!*

When I first read *The Power of Your Subconscious Mind* by Joseph Murphy, I thought surely just doing as he recommends was too simple. It couldn't be that easy. But what did I have to lose? I'd already lost nearly all of my material possessions, so I might as well give it a try.

And I did.

Now, nearly 20 years later, I'm grateful beyond measure for finding Joseph Murphy's little passage in his book, which I refer to as, "The Wealth Exercise." I have used this exercise to:

- manifest promotions and raises, taking my corporate career from an entry level technology position to vice president
- begin a savings fund from nothing and grow it large enough to pay for my magnificent wedding without touching my substantial emergency fund, which I'd also grown from zero
- rent ideal apartments and eventually purchase my dream home
- and much more…

More important than all of those *things* has been the attainment of an immeasurable inner wealth, contentment and peace. Doing "The Wealth Exercise" consistently for all these years has also helped me create amazing relationships and experience great joy.

And, I wish all of that for you as well.

Now as a Business and Life Coach, I give this exercise regularly to clients. I originally designed this journal for them, but I wanted to share what I know with everyone who desires to experience greater health, wealth, happiness and success in their lives. I am so grateful this journal has found its way to you.

I only ask one thing of you. Okay, two things. First, that you commit to doing "The Wealth Exercise" for at least six to eight weeks. This is an eight week journal to assist you in creating and solidifying a new habit of thinking wealth thoughts. If you are in debt, or experiencing lack of any kind, you didn't get here overnight. In most cases, it took years, even decades to create your current circumstances. We need a bit of time to make and see the changes that this exercise offers.

If you are not in debt but have stalled in any area of your life, use this exercise to break through the wall between where you are now to experience even greater success.

The second request is to continue doing "The Wealth Exercise" for the rest of your life. Again, this exercise is about more than your material desires. It grows as you grow. Play with it and have fun with it.

I'm not asking you to journal forever…although feel free to as it can assist with lasting and continual improvements. Doing the exercise consistently, even just inwardly, will help create the habit of thinking of and believing in wealth and can lead to incremental shifts that could provide huge long-term benefits. Just commit to taking a few minutes, even as short as just 30 seconds, each day and using the word "wealth."

The Inside Out Approach to Wealth

"The Wealth Exercise" is designed to raise your vibration and to change you from the inside out. Every *thing* has a vibration, a resonance. The vibration is the feeling of that thing. A small apartment has a particular feel while a larger one might have a more expansive feel, and a house a different feeling altogether.

This journal is designed to help you get into the *feeling* of what you want to experience next in your life, whether it's a new job, a new car, a new home, etc. Getting into the feeling of whatever you desire will begin to raise your resonance with that desire. You will begin to own it from the inside out, grow in your comfort with the idea of that desire, and ultimately it can come into your reality.

One client who was working on feeling more comfortable with making more money came up with the creative idea to see the word *wealth* in her meditation as a DNA strand. She saw it changing her at the cellular level, allowing her to see new possibilities for her life and to believe that they were, in fact, possible.

How to Use the *Wealth Transformation Journal*

Select a *Wealth* Intention

This journal is designed to be used over the next 60 days. Begin by selecting something you would like to manifest in your life, such as a promotion with a raise (I recommend seeing them both together), a new car, a new home, a romantic partner, or even new friends if you are feeling lonely, etc. Write down what you'd like to experience in the *My Wealth Intentions* section. Be as specific as you would like. If there are several things you'd like to manifest, choose one, no more than two, ideas to focus on at a time. Having too many things to focus on can scatter you and diminish your results.

Make it 50% Believable

Here's a point of clarification on "The Wealth Exercise." One of the things I learned while getting my Masters of Spiritual Psychology from the University of Santa Monica, is that when going for a goal or a dream, make it at least 50% believable.

I once had a client that I'd given "The Wealth Exercise" to who was still struggling financially sometime later. I asked her if she was doing the exercise and she exclaimed, "Oh yes!" Her enthusiasm sparked some concern given her circumstances so I asked her to share what she was visualizing. She went on to detail a vault with pallets of money and gold bouillon and shelves of jewels and other riches. When I inquired if her vision was believable, she said yes. I then asked if it were possible within the next month or even six months, within her realm of control and opportunities? She fell silent and after some time said, "No."

Choose a goal that is 50% believable and, I dare say reasonable within your sphere of influence. If you don't have any discretionary money at the end of the month after paying all minimum balances, rent, utilities, etc., see yourself paying all minimums and having $50-$100 extra at the end of the month. Once you attain that goal, or get close, bump that vision up to $500 extra at the end of the month, then $1,000, etc. If you would like a promotion and you're making $40,000/year, visualizing making $120,000 may not be helpful or effective. Choose $60,000-$70,000 per year first.

What I have found that has worked for clients and myself is to stair step the way up the vibrational ladder of wealth. This can help you move to a new level of wealth, experience it, live into it, and hold that new level. Then you can rinse and repeat, doing the same process over and over again.

Many people who suddenly come into great sums of money do not do well long-term, and even experience great tragedy and loss. While you may want to go quicker, enjoy the wins as you go, experiencing the confidence that comes from knowing that you have the power to do this repeatedly.

And whether you believe in Karma or not, there is a reciprocal law to the Universe, which is what I lovingly refer to as the Boomerang Effect. Any malice or judgment against another or even coveting what someone else has can have less than ideal results and demonstrates lack thinking. There is enough wealth, love, peace, and joy for all of us in this world. We need not try to take it from others. If we do, it can be taken from us.

Do not put your energy and focus with "The Wealth Exercise" into attracting what someone else has. Choose your intentions such that what you desire does not harm another. Again, connect inside to the essence and the qualities of what you desire and allow God, the Universe, etc., to bring that to you for the highest good of all concerned.

Identify the Wealth Qualities

One key I have found for attracting sustainable increases in wealth is to connect to the qualities of the thing I want to experience. After you've written out your intention(s), go to the *Wealth Qualities* section of this journal. There you will find a starter list of words that describe the feeling of wealth.

Feel free to write in other words that resonate with you as well. It is extremely important to identify the qualities that you want to experience as they will help you know inside when the *thing* you desire arrives.

You may think, I will feel happy when it arrives because the car will be parked in my driveway or I'll be making more money. But have you ever wanted something, got it and then didn't like it or didn't want it anymore? Chances are you may not have been in touch with the experience you wanted from it. Knowing the qualities also helps with clarity. An example might be that you want a new home or apartment. The qualities you could be looking for are expansiveness and spaciousness. As you do "the Wealth Exercise," you may begin to notice there is clutter in your home and suddenly you hear of a book like *The Life-Changing Magic of Tidying Up* (which I highly recommend), and you read it and get rid of all your clutter. Upon completion, you look around at the openness and feel a new sense of expansiveness and spaciousness in your existing apartment, without moving.

There is a new quote and a *Wealth Intention* page to start each week of this 8-week journal. Each week, write out a summary of your intention on the page provided. Review the *Wealth Qualities* page and identify the qualities you want to experience more that week. It is absolutely okay to keep the same ones week to week, or you may choose new ones. This will help you connect more deeply with what you'd like to experience and enhance your focus and clarity.

Using the Wealth Meditation Each Day

For a few moments each morning, get a picture in your mind of what you desire and what that might look AND feel like. Say the word wealth over and over again to yourself silently and get into the feeling of what it would feel like to experience that thing in your life.

Joseph Murphy uses the words "Wealth. Success." in the passage I quote from *The Power of Your Subconscious Mind*. Personally, I have chosen to use just the word "Wealth." I found for myself, and similarly for my clients, that I can only hold one focus in my mind at a time. I have therefore included success in my personal definition of wealth. You can do the same or use both words, or use another word such as Health if that is what you desire.

I have a dear friend, Felicia Slattery, who I shared this technique with when she told me she had been diagnosed with lung cancer. Felicia did everything on the mental, emotional, physical and spiritual levels to heal herself and used the word Health. Felicia asked for prayer and prayed, she had surgery, and she changed her mindset, and she is now cancer free.

> **DISCLAIMER:** the inclusion of Felicia's story is not to be taken as medical advice…nor any other information shared as financial advice or otherwise. Please use sound judgment and get whatever assistance available and necessary for your situation.

Another example of how to use this exercise is from my own life in how I manifested many of my job promotions. Whenever I felt I was ready for a promotion, each morning I would use the word *wealth* over and over again in my mind, silently, to get into what it would feel like to be at the next level in my career. I would envision changing my email signature at the company I worked for at that time to include my new title. I pictured in my mind coworkers hearing of my promotion and genuinely congratulating me and telling me it was well deserved. Most importantly, I envisioned myself performing in my new role and noticing what I would be doing differently and how that felt.

Taking Action

Now, you may have recognized that "The Wealth Exercise" seems very similar to the Law of Attraction, and in fact it does intentionally utilize that law. However, "The Wealth Exercise" stresses an important element that is often forgotten by teachers of the Law of Attraction.

You may have heard that if you think about something long enough, it will happen. But what I've discovered is that it is the *inspired ideas* that come to mind during meditation and taking action on those ideas that accelerate the manifestation process. Inspiration in meditation could look like someone coming to mind to call or email, getting the idea to apply to a school, seeing yourself creating a special report on a project you're working on and presenting to the leadership team, scheduling a one-on-one with the boss to talk about new opportunities to showcase your talents, etc. These are the very things that came to mind in my meditations. I took action on those inspired ideas right away, most times that day, and they helped catapult me to success.

My business clients often report that their meditations reveal new products and services to offer their clients, special ways to work with particular clients, and multitudes of ways to add value in their business. And when they followed through on these inspirations, it was amazing to see how the Universe supported them with extraordinary success.

So, each morning, do the exercise for a few minutes to connect to the feeling of what you want to experience. Write down anything that comes forward in the *Meditation Inspiration* section for that day. Then wear the idea of your desire throughout your day, like a beloved coat. What would you be thinking about if you already had that promotion you want? What would it feel like to really be driving that new car or putting the keys into the lock and opening the door of your new home? What would it feel like to be in a great relationship or to have a wonderful new friend, and how would you be a great partner or friend to them?

Write down any actions to take in the *Action Items* section. Follow through on inspired ideas that come forward that day. If you've set an intention for a new car, pay attention to questions and ideas that arise like,

- check your credit score
- do you have enough in savings to buy the car outright
- do you know the trade-in value of your current car
- have you looked into buying programs like with a credit union, AAA or Costco
- have you test driven different cars

The list above is not exhaustive as there are many things you could do to prepare. When I was moving up in cars after the bankruptcy, I had the courage to talk to a woman at the credit union I belonged to. I say courage because I had to be willing to share with another person the truth of my former situation. She was wonderful! She asked me to hold off from buying a car for six more months and advised me to pay my credit cards down. She said that if I could do that, I would be able to qualify for a good interest rate. And, she was right! I qualified for a "normal" person's interest rate with good credit just months later.

The goal is not to go into debt or to purchase beyond your means. If you take out a loan, use "The Wealth Exercise" to see it paid in full well ahead of time.

At the end of your day, check off any action items completed. Add any notes to the *Observations of the Day* section about how wealth is starting to show up in your life, i.e., did someone buy you coffee or lunch, did you find a penny or even a dime on the street [hint: I take that to mean God, the Universe, whatever is throwing money at your feet], did you pay off a debt, etc. Pay attention to the little and the big ways money is showing up in your life. And again, take action on those inspired ideas that come forward.

Let your imagination soar in the *Doodles and Daydreams* section. Draw, paste pictures, cutout words, whatever you would like. Give your creativity a place to expand in this area.

Gratitude & Wealth

The feeling of wealth also includes gratitude. Gratitude for what is now, as well as for what you are asking the Universe for in the future. Putting on the coat of what you desire opens up the opportunity to feel and be grateful for the experience of here and now. And remember, you are going toward your next level of wealth. As you're doing the exercise and feeling into the wealth of what you desire, connect also to the gratitude you will feel when that *thing* arrives.

Years ago, I was living a bit of a hermit's life working 50-60 hours per week with very little social interaction. My only close friend who I went to movies and events with moved out of state. I found myself quite lonely and decided I wanted to find new friends nearby to socialize with. I set the intention and used "The Wealth Exercise" to feel into what it would be like to have more friends. I wanted to find people who I loved being around, who loved me, and to whom I could be a good friend to as well. During my meditations, I felt the gratitude for their friendship, whoever they would be. Within a few months, I met a woman at a workshop who lived in a neighboring town and she introduced me to two of her friends. The four of us became life long friends. These women are spectacular and the gratitude I feel today for them and their kindness, caring, loving and extraordinary friendship began with that intention.

An easy way to incorporate gratitude into your process is to simply circle the word "Gratitude" on the Wealth Qualities page and add it in the weekly qualities section. Just that connection to gratitude can assist in raising your vibration to the wealth you would like to experience next in your life.

Let's Get Started

Use "The Wealth Exercise" and this *Wealth Transformation Journal* to track your progress, capture your inspired ideas and take action to experience greater inner wealth and, therefore, greater outer wealth.

Wealth *is* an inside game. It starts with how we feel about ourselves and the opportunities presented to us. It only takes a few moments a day to begin to feel into wealth in a new and expanded way.

Please visit http://www.KaminSamuel.com/wealthsuccess to watch videos on wealth, share your successes, ask questions, and get additional resources to assist you with your quest for increased wealth and success.

I wish you abundant success!

Summary *Wealth* Checklist

1. Read "The Wealth Exercise" again from *The Power of Your Subconscious Mind* by Joseph Murphy.

2. In the *My Wealth Intentions* section, write down anything you would like to manifest in your life, i.e., attracting more money into your life, getting promoted, improving your health, creating a relationship, experiencing more success, etc. Write down what you would like to experience. Make sure it's at least 50% believable. Choose one to focus on over the next eight weeks.

3. Turn to the *Wealth Qualities* page and circle the qualities that best represent what you would like to experience through receiving your intention. Feel free to write in additional qualities that resonate with you.

4. Beginning with the *Week 1 Wealth Intention*, rewrite your intention succinctly and add the corresponding qualities for that week.

5. Each morning do "The Wealth Exercise" for at least 30 seconds, ideally a few minutes. It doesn't take long to begin raising your vibration. Ask yourself, "what would it feel like to have..." Get into the *feeling* of what you want.

6. Keep your journal nearby. Write down any inspirations or ideas that come forward, i.e., to call or email someone, get your resume together, make an appointment of some kind, etc. Write down actions to take in the Action Items section.

7. Take action that day and watch what magic can happen.

8. Before drifting off to sleep, check off any completed Action Items from the day. Then, note any observations you've had. Did you receive wealth of any kind, i.e., did you take your car in for service and it was less than expected, did you find a dime on the street, did someone buy you lunch or even a coffee, did you get a raise, etc. Wealth comes in many forms. What happened when you followed through on your action items? We want to notice it all, especially the small indications that we are stepping into a new flow in our lives.

9. Note any images that come forward in the Doodles and Daydream section. You can paste pictures, cutout words, draw, whatever you would like. Let your imagination soar.

10. Visit http://www.KaminSamuel.com/wealthsuccess for instructions on how to get support, watch videos on "The Wealth Exercise," share your wins, and much more.

11. HAVE FUN. Step into the flow of experiencing more wealth and success in your life today. Enjoy!

Part 2 - The Journal

Once the subconscious mind accepts an idea, it begins to execute it.

Joseph Murphy

My *Wealth* Intentions

Today's Date: _____

_____

_____

_____

_____

_____

_____

_____

_____

_____

_____

Wealth **Qualities**

Abundance	Gratitude	Prosperous
Affluent	Grandeur	Radiance
Authenticity	Harmony	Rich
Bliss	Health	Safety
Bountiful	Inspired	Security
Confidence	Joy	Splendor
Creativity	Luxurious	Strength
Dependability	Magnificence	Successful
Flourishing	Opulence	Thriving
Freedom	Peace	Vivacious
Generous	Playfulness	Wealth
Grace	Profitable	_____

"The biggest adventure you
can take is to live the life
of your dreams."
Oprah Winfrey

Wealth

Week 1 Wealth Intention

Week of: _____

_____

_____

_____

_____

_____

Qualities

_____

_____

_____

_____

_____

Date: _____

Meditation Inspirations

_____

_____

_____

_____

_____

_____

_____

Action Items

☐ _____

☐ _____

☐ _____

☐ _____

☐ _____

☐ _____

Observations of the Day

_____

_____

_____

_____

_____

_____

_____

Doodles & Daydreams

Date: _____

Meditation Inspirations

_____

_____

_____

_____

_____

_____

_____

Action Items

☐ _____

☐ _____

☐ _____

☐ _____

☐ _____

☐ _____

Wealth

Observations of the Day

_____

_____

_____

_____

_____

_____

_____

Doodles & Daydreams

Date: _____

Meditation Inspirations

_____

_____

_____

_____

_____

_____

_____

Action Items

❑ _____

❑ _____

❑ _____

❑ _____

❑ _____

❑ _____

Observations of the Day

_____

_____

_____

_____

_____

_____

_____

_____

Doodles & Daydreams

Date: _____

Meditation Inspirations

_____

_____

_____

_____

_____

_____

_____

Action Items

❑ _____

❑ _____

❑ _____

❑ _____

❑ _____

❑ _____

Observations of the Day

_____

_____

_____

_____

_____

_____

_____

_____

Doodles & Daydreams

Date: _____

Meditation Inspirations

_____

_____

_____

_____

_____

_____

_____

Action Items

☐ _____

☐ _____

☐ _____

☐ _____

☐ _____

☐ _____

Wealth

Observations of the Day

_____

_____

_____

_____

_____

_____

_____

_____

Doodles & Daydreams

Date: _____

Meditation Inspirations

_____

_____

_____

_____

_____

_____

_____

Action Items

☐ _____

☐ _____

☐ _____

☐ _____

☐ _____

☐ _____

Observations of the Day

Doodles & Daydreams

Date: _____

Meditation Inspirations

_____

_____

_____

_____

_____

_____

_____

Action Items

❑ _____

❑ _____

❑ _____

❑ _____

❑ _____

❑ _____

Wealth

Observations of the Day

_____

_____

_____

_____

_____

_____

_____

Doodles & Daydreams

Wealth

"Once your thoughts reflect what you genuinely want to be, the appropriate emotions and the consequent behavior will flow automatically. Believe it, and you will see it!"
Wayne Dyer

Wealth

Week 2 Wealth Intention

Week of: _____

_____

_____

_____

_____

_____

Qualities

_____

_____

_____

_____

_____

Date: _____

Meditation Inspirations

_____

_____

_____

_____

_____

_____

_____

_____

Action Items

☐ _____

☐ _____

☐ _____

☐ _____

☐ _____

☐ _____

Wealth

Observations of the Day

_____

_____

_____

_____

_____

_____

_____

Doodles & Daydreams

Date: _____

Meditation Inspirations

_____

_____

_____

_____

_____

_____

_____

Action Items

❑ _____

❑ _____

❑ _____

❑ _____

❑ _____

❑ _____

Observations of the Day

_____

_____

_____

_____

_____

_____

_____

_____

Doodles & Daydreams

Date: _____

Meditation Inspirations

_____

_____

_____

_____

_____

_____

_____

Action Items

❑ _____

❑ _____

❑ _____

❑ _____

❑ _____

❑ _____

Observations of the Day

_____

_____

_____

_____

_____

_____

_____

Doodles & Daydreams

Date: _____

Meditation Inspirations

_____

_____

_____

_____

_____

_____

_____

Action Items

☐ _____

☐ _____

☐ _____

☐ _____

☐ _____

☐ _____

Wealth

Observations of the Day

_____

_____

_____

_____

_____

_____

_____

_____

Doodles & Daydreams

Wealth

Date: _____

Meditation Inspirations

_____

_____

_____

_____

_____

_____

_____

Action Items

☐ _____

☐ _____

☐ _____

☐ _____

☐ _____

☐ _____

Observations of the Day

_____

_____

_____

_____

_____

_____

_____

Doodles & Daydreams

Date: _____

Meditation Inspirations

_____

_____

_____

_____

_____

_____

_____

Action Items

❑ _____

❑ _____

❑ _____

❑ _____

❑ _____

❑ _____

Observations of the Day

_____

_____

_____

_____

_____

_____

_____

Doodles & Daydreams

Date: _____

Meditation Inspirations

_____

_____

_____

_____

_____

_____

_____

Action Items

❑   _____

❑   _____

❑   _____

❑   _____

❑   _____

❑   _____

Observations of the Day

_____

_____

_____

_____

_____

_____

_____

Doodles & Daydreams

"The future belongs to those who believe in the beauty of their dreams."

Eleanor Roosevelt

Wealth

Week 3 Wealth Intention

Week of: _____

_____

_____

_____

_____

_____

Qualities

_____

_____

_____

_____

Date: _____

Meditation Inspirations

_____

_____

_____

_____

_____

_____

_____

Action Items

☐ _____

☐ _____

☐ _____

☐ _____

☐ _____

☐ _____

Wealth

Observations of the Day

_____

_____

_____

_____

_____

_____

_____

Doodles & Daydreams

Wealth

Date: _____

Meditation Inspirations

_____

_____

_____

_____

_____

_____

_____

Action Items

☐ _____

☐ _____

☐ _____

☐ _____

☐ _____

☐ _____

Wealth

Observations of the Day

_____

_____

_____

_____

_____

_____

_____

_____

Doodles & Daydreams

Date: _____

Meditation Inspirations

_____

_____

_____

_____

_____

_____

_____

Action Items

❑ _____

❑ _____

❑ _____

❑ _____

❑ _____

❑ _____

Observations of the Day

_____

_____

_____

_____

_____

_____

_____

Doodles & Daydreams

Date: _____

Meditation Inspirations

_____

_____

_____

_____

_____

_____

_____

Action Items

❑ _____

❑ _____

❑ _____

❑ _____

❑ _____

❑ _____

Observations of the Day

_____

_____

_____

_____

_____

_____

_____

Doodles & Daydreams

Date: _____

Meditation Inspirations

_____

_____

_____

_____

_____

_____

_____

Action Items

❑ _____

❑ _____

❑ _____

❑ _____

❑ _____

❑ _____

Observations of the Day

_____

_____

_____

_____

_____

_____

_____

_____

Doodles & Daydreams

Wealth

Date: _____

Meditation Inspirations

_____

_____

_____

_____

_____

_____

_____

Action Items

❑ _____

❑ _____

❑ _____

❑ _____

❑ _____

❑ _____

Wealth

Observations of the Day

Doodles & Daydreams

Date: _____

Meditation Inspirations

_____

_____

_____

_____

_____

_____

_____

Action Items

❑ _____

❑ _____

❑ _____

❑ _____

❑ _____

❑ _____

Wealth

Observations of the Day

_____

_____

_____

_____

_____

_____

_____

_____

Doodles & Daydreams

"The soul attracts that which it secretly harbors; that which it loves, and also that which it fears."

James Allen

Wealth

Week 4 Wealth Intention

Week of: _____

_____

_____

_____

_____

Qualities

_____

_____

_____

_____

Date: _____

Meditation Inspirations

_____

_____

_____

_____

_____

_____

_____

Action Items

❑ _____

❑ _____

❑ _____

❑ _____

❑ _____

❑ _____

Observations of the Day

_____

_____

_____

_____

_____

_____

_____

Doodles & Daydreams

Date: _____

Meditation Inspirations

_____

_____

_____

_____

_____

_____

_____

Action Items

❑   _____

❑   _____

❑   _____

❑   _____

❑   _____

❑   _____

Observations of the Day

_____

_____

_____

_____

_____

_____

_____

Doodles & Daydreams

Date: _____

Meditation Inspirations

_____

_____

_____

_____

_____

_____

_____

Action Items

❑ _____

❑ _____

❑ _____

❑ _____

❑ _____

❑ _____

Observations of the Day

_____

_____

_____

_____

_____

_____

_____

Doodles & Daydreams

Date: _____

Meditation Inspirations

_____

_____

_____

_____

_____

_____

_____

Action Items

❑ _____

❑ _____

❑ _____

❑ _____

❑ _____

❑ _____

Observations of the Day

_____

_____

_____

_____

_____

_____

_____

Doodles & Daydreams

Wealth

Date: _____

Meditation Inspirations

_____

_____

_____

_____

_____

_____

_____

Action Items

❑ _____

❑ _____

❑ _____

❑ _____

❑ _____

❑ _____

Observations of the Day

_____

_____

_____

_____

_____

_____

_____

Doodles & Daydreams

Date: _____

Meditation Inspirations

_____

_____

_____

_____

_____

_____

_____

Action Items

❑ _____

❑ _____

❑ _____

❑ _____

❑ _____

❑ _____

Wealth

Observations of the Day

_____

_____

_____

_____

_____

_____

_____

Doodles & Daydreams

Wealth

Date: _____

Meditation Inspirations

_____

_____

_____

_____

_____

_____

_____

Action Items

❏ _____

❏ _____

❏ _____

❏ _____

❏ _____

❏ _____

Wealth

Observations of the Day

_____

_____

_____

_____

_____

_____

_____

Doodles & Daydreams

"What you seek is seeking you."
Rumi

Wealth

Week 5 Wealth Intention

Week of: _____

_____

_____

_____

_____

_____

Qualities

_____

_____

_____

_____

_____

Date: _____

Meditation Inspirations

_____

_____

_____

_____

_____

_____

_____

Action Items

☐ _____

☐ _____

☐ _____

☐ _____

☐ _____

☐ _____

Observations of the Day

_____

_____

_____

_____

_____

_____

_____

Doodles & Daydreams

Date: _____

Meditation Inspirations

_____

_____

_____

_____

_____

_____

_____

Action Items

❑ _____

❑ _____

❑ _____

❑ _____

❑ _____

❑ _____

Observations of the Day

_____

_____

_____

_____

_____

_____

_____

Doodles & Daydreams

Wealth

Date: _____

Meditation Inspirations

_____

_____

_____

_____

_____

_____

_____

_____

Action Items

❏ _____

❏ _____

❏ _____

❏ _____

❏ _____

❏ _____

Observations of the Day

Doodles & Daydreams

Date: _____

Meditation Inspirations

_____

_____

_____

_____

_____

_____

_____

Action Items

❏ _____

❏ _____

❏ _____

❏ _____

❏ _____

❏ _____

Observations of the Day

_____

_____

_____

_____

_____

_____

_____

Doodles & Daydreams

Date: _____

Meditation Inspirations

_____

_____

_____

_____

_____

_____

_____

Action Items

❑ _____

❑ _____

❑ _____

❑ _____

❑ _____

❑ _____

Wealth

Observations of the Day

_____

_____

_____

_____

_____

_____

_____

Doodles & Daydreams

Date: _____

Meditation Inspirations

_____

_____

_____

_____

_____

_____

_____

Action Items

❑   _____

❑   _____

❑   _____

❑   _____

❑   _____

❑   _____

Observations of the Day

_____

_____

_____

_____

_____

_____

_____

Doodles & Daydreams

Date: _____

Meditation Inspirations

_____

_____

_____

_____

_____

_____

_____

Action Items

❑ _____

❑ _____

❑ _____

❑ _____

❑ _____

❑ _____

Wealth

Observations of the Day

_____

_____

_____

_____

_____

_____

_____

Doodles & Daydreams

"The world needs dreamers and the world needs doers. But above all, the world needs dreamers who do."
Sarah Ban Breathnach

Week 6 Wealth Intention

Week of: _____

_____

_____

_____

_____

Qualities

_____

_____

_____

_____

_____

Date: _____

Meditation Inspirations

_____

_____

_____

_____

_____

_____

_____

Action Items

❑ _____

❑ _____

❑ _____

❑ _____

❑ _____

❑ _____

Observations of the Day

_____

_____

_____

_____

_____

_____

Doodles & Daydreams

Date: _____

Meditation Inspirations

_____

_____

_____

_____

_____

_____

_____

Action Items

❏ _____

❏ _____

❏ _____

❏ _____

❏ _____

❏ _____

Observations of the Day

_____

_____

_____

_____

_____

_____

_____

Doodles & Daydreams

Date: _____

Meditation Inspirations

_____

_____

_____

_____

_____

_____

_____

Action Items

❏ _____

❏ _____

❏ _____

❏ _____

❏ _____

❏ _____

Observations of the Day

_____

_____

_____

_____

_____

_____

_____

Doodles & Daydreams

Date: _____

Meditation Inspirations

_____

_____

_____

_____

_____

_____

_____

Action Items

- ❑ _____
- ❑ _____
- ❑ _____
- ❑ _____
- ❑ _____
- ❑ _____

Observations of the Day

_____

_____

_____

_____

_____

_____

_____

Doodles & Daydreams

Date: _____

Meditation Inspirations

_____

_____

_____

_____

_____

_____

_____

Action Items

❑ _____

❑ _____

❑ _____

❑ _____

❑ _____

❑ _____

Wealth

Observations of the Day

_____

_____

_____

_____

_____

_____

_____

Doodles & Daydreams

Date: _____

Meditation Inspirations

_____

_____

_____

_____

_____

_____

_____

Action Items

❑ _____

❑ _____

❑ _____

❑ _____

❑ _____

❑ _____

Wealth

Observations of the Day

_____

_____

_____

_____

_____

_____

_____

Doodles & Daydreams

Date: _____

Meditation Inspirations

_____

_____

_____

_____

_____

_____

_____

Action Items

☐   _____

☐   _____

☐   _____

☐   _____

☐   _____

☐   _____

Observations of the Day

_____

_____

_____

_____

_____

_____

_____

Doodles & Daydreams

"You must find the place inside yourself where nothing is impossible."
Deepak Chopra

Wealth

Week 7 Wealth Intention

Week of: _____

_____

_____

_____

_____

_____

Qualities

_____

_____

_____

_____

_____

Date: _____

Meditation Inspirations

_____

_____

_____

_____

_____

_____

_____

Action Items

❑   _____

❑   _____

❑   _____

❑   _____

❑   _____

❑   _____

Observations of the Day

_____

_____

_____

_____

_____

_____

_____

Doodles & Daydreams

Date: _____

Meditation Inspirations

_____

_____

_____

_____

_____

_____

_____

_____

Action Items

☐ _____

☐ _____

☐ _____

☐ _____

☐ _____

☐ _____

Wealth

Observations of the Day

_____

_____

_____

_____

_____

_____

_____

Doodles & Daydreams

Date: _____

Meditation Inspirations

_____

_____

_____

_____

_____

_____

_____

Action Items

❑ _____

❑ _____

❑ _____

❑ _____

❑ _____

❑ _____

Observations of the Day

_____

_____

_____

_____

_____

_____

_____

Doodles & Daydreams

Date: _____

Meditation Inspirations

_____

_____

_____

_____

_____

_____

_____

Action Items

❑ _____

❑ _____

❑ _____

❑ _____

❑ _____

❑ _____

Observations of the Day

_____

_____

_____

_____

_____

_____

_____

Doodles & Daydreams

Date: _____

Meditation Inspirations

_____

_____

_____

_____

_____

_____

_____

Action Items

❑ _____

❑ _____

❑ _____

❑ _____

❑ _____

❑ _____

Wealth

Observations of the Day

_____

_____

_____

_____

_____

_____

_____

Doodles & Daydreams

Date: _____

Meditation Inspirations

_____

_____

_____

_____

_____

_____

_____

Action Items

❑ _____

❑ _____

❑ _____

❑ _____

❑ _____

❑ _____

Observations of the Day

_____

_____

_____

_____

_____

_____

_____

Doodles & Daydreams

Date: _____

Meditation Inspirations

_____

_____

_____

_____

_____

_____

_____

Action Items

❑ _____

❑ _____

❑ _____

❑ _____

❑ _____

❑ _____

Observations of the Day

_____

_____

_____

_____

_____

_____

_____

Doodles & Daydreams

"We ask ourselves, who am I to be brilliant, gorgeous, handsome, talented and fabulous? Actually, who are you not to be?"
Marianne Williamson

Week 8 Wealth Intention

Week of: _____

_____

_____

_____

_____

_____

Qualities

_____

_____

_____

_____

_____

Date: _____

Meditation Inspirations

_____

_____

_____

_____

_____

_____

_____

Action Items

❑ _____

❑ _____

❑ _____

❑ _____

❑ _____

❑ _____

Observations of the Day

_____

_____

_____

_____

_____

_____

_____

Doodles & Daydreams

Date: _____

Meditation Inspirations

_____

_____

_____

_____

_____

_____

_____

_____

Action Items

❑ _____

❑ _____

❑ _____

❑ _____

❑ _____

❑ _____

Observations of the Day

_____

_____

_____

_____

_____

_____

_____

Doodles & Daydreams

Date: _____

Meditation Inspirations

_____

_____

_____

_____

_____

_____

_____

_____

Action Items

❑   _____

❑   _____

❑   _____

❑   _____

❑   _____

❑   _____

Observations of the Day

_____

_____

_____

_____

_____

_____

_____

Doodles & Daydreams

Date: _____

Meditation Inspirations

_____

_____

_____

_____

_____

_____

_____

Action Items

☐ _____

☐ _____

☐ _____

☐ _____

☐ _____

☐ _____

Observations of the Day

_____

_____

_____

_____

_____

_____

_____

Doodles & Daydreams

Date: _____

Meditation Inspirations

_____
_____
_____
_____
_____
_____
_____
_____

Action Items

☐ _____

☐ _____

☐ _____

☐ _____

☐ _____

☐ _____

Wealth

Observations of the Day

_____

_____

_____

_____

_____

_____

_____

Doodles & Daydreams

Date: _____

Meditation Inspirations

_____

_____

_____

_____

_____

_____

_____

Action Items

❑ _____

❑ _____

❑ _____

❑ _____

❑ _____

❑ _____

Observations of the Day

_____

_____

_____

_____

_____

_____

_____

Doodles & Daydreams

Wealth

Date: _____

Meditation Inspirations

_____

_____

_____

_____

_____

_____

_____

_____

Action Items

❏ _____

❏ _____

❏ _____

❏ _____

❏ _____

❏ _____

Observations of the Day

_____

_____

_____

_____

_____

_____

Doodles & Daydreams

"On your death bed, you will not wish you had been more comfortable, or that you had found an even easier, softer pleasure zone to hide out in. You will wish you had ventured out more. That you had spoken up more. Tried some things. Reinvented yourself one more time."

Steve Chandler

Notes

Notes

Notes

Notes

Notes

About the Author

Kamin Samuel started her professional career as the U.S. Navy's first female African-American helicopter pilot. She transitioned to having several small businesses and then to corporate as a web developer at a computer electronics company. Kamin moved up quickly working for several organizations, even serving as a Vice President of Global Website Operations at a billion dollar company.

Kamin is now an international business and career coach and strategist helping professionals increase their wealth mindset, improve performance, develop leadership skills, and create strategies to expand their opportunities. She assists her clients in identifying and clearing their inner blocks to achieving greater success in all areas of their lives.

Working closely with Kamin, her clients double, even quadruple businesses, gain greater clarity on life purpose, explore new opportunities for their next phase of life, receive promotions and raises, start or deepen relationships, and receive extraordinary support during/after loss of parents and healing past issues and reconceiving themselves in the world.

Kamin holds a Masters of Science in Information Systems, a Masters of Arts in Spiritual Psychology, and a Masters of Science in Spiritual Science. Kamin's unique background combines the technical and soft skills, allowing her to assist individuals in taking practical action in the real world that gets dramatic results.

Kamin lives in California with her husband Mark.

You can learn more and watch informative videos on transforming your business, career and life by visiting her website, www.KaminSamuel.com and signing up for the *Wealth Breakthrough Kit* today!

Made in the USA
Lexington, KY
23 October 2019

55888350R00098